WHERE THE
LYREBIRD LIVES
VIKKI CONLEY • MAX HAMILTON

Windy Hollow Books

For the lyrebirds who live in Tarra Valley
and Tarra-Bulga National Park. VC

For Adam, Maggie, Declan and Bridget. MH

Vikki Conley is a CBCA short-listed author with multiple internationally published picture books. Vikki is a nature lover, intrepid traveller, and passionate spotter of rarely sighted animals like lyrebirds, platypus and bower birds. She writes children's stories that celebrate the spirit of wonder, adventure, and freedom that she wishes every child could enjoy.

Max Hamilton is an award-winning illustrator, graphic designer and most enthusiastically a maker of children's books. She enjoys noticing the little details in things, loves to get lost in the world of illustration and stories, and through her art aims to raise awareness of the importance of protecting our Australian fauna.

First published in hardback in 2022
by Windy Hollow Books

PO Box 265, Kew East, Victoria, Australia 3102
www.windyhollowbooks.com.au
www.facebook.com/windyhollowbooks

ISBN: 9780645323566 (hardback)
Design by Nuovo Group

A catalogue record for this
book is available from the
National Library of Australia

Today we're going
to where the lyrebird lives.

Will we see him?
I don't know.

But if we don't tip-toe,
we definitely won't.

High in the mountains
through the sleepy clouds.

Deep in the forest
past the chiming birds.

Pop says lyrebirds
mimic what they hear,
trilling to themselves.

Shhh,

listen with your ears.

Wisha-wisha trees

that dance with the sun.

Clitter-clatter bridge
that swings in the wind.

Listen can you hear?
Is that his sound?

Koo-koo. Kaa-kaa.

I wonder if that's him?

Nanna says he dances
with his feathers up high,
over in the gully.

Shall we go look there?

Over the river that
babbles like a bird.

Down in the gully
past the giant
lace ferns.

Listen can you hear?
Is that his sound?

Wwww-hip, chirp.

I wonder if that's him?

Mamma says he drinks
at the base of the fall,
sipping with his beak.

Quick! Let's go there.

Careful on the log,
over frog green moss.

Slippery and wet.

Shimmy, shimmy...

Hop!

Listen can you hear?
Is that his sound?

Cheep-ity
cheep.

I wonder if that's him?

Daddy says he scratches with his claws in the leaves, hunting for grubs. Has he just been here?

Will we see the lyrebird?

Tip-toe tip-toe...